God I need to talk to You about Internet Activity

Michael Newman

CONCORDIA PUBLISHING HOUSE · SAINT LOUIS

3558 S. Jefferson Avenue, St. Louis, MO 63118-3968
1-800-325-3040 · www.cph.org

Written by Michael Newman

Manufactured in the United States of America

1 2 3 4 5 6 7 8 9 10 22 21 20 19 18 17 16 15 14 13

Table of CONTENTS

A note to the reader: Some of the details in these prayers may not reflect your unique situation. Therefore, we encourage you to adapt them where appropriate to fit your circumstances and spiritual needs.

Introduction

The Internet is a wonderful and powerful tool. The information and opportunities it makes accessible boggle the mind. Like all human inventions—money, the printing press, medicine, and entertainment, to name a few—today's Internet technology can be used for our good and for God's glory. Or not.

Satan delights in distorting our use of neutral things until they become portals to wickedness. He does a happy dance when the Internet distracts us from who we are as God's children. And to make matters worse, our own physiological make-up seems to encourage sinful behavior when our brain chemistry changes to the extent that it depends on technology-fired pleasure centers.

The technology is new, but the problem is not. From the first sin via that proverbial apple, to the latest search results, anything that compels us to displace God from the center of our lives is sinful. When we put our own pleasure first, we become our own god and the gift of technology becomes our idol.

We don't want this. We want to live God-pleasing lives. We know that all sin, secret or otherwise, is an abomination to our Lord. And we despise ourselves for our weakness. But we can't help it; the thrill is almost irresistible. Our devices make it so easy.

Besides, a little bit won't hurt, will it? Just one more time? For a minute or two? No one else will know. We sneak a peek at images that would otherwise offend. We waste time or even avoid responsibilities with the latest game or off-color social media post. We are so accustomed to being logged on that if Internet access is unavailable, we grow anxious and irritable. We *have* to check our e-mail, play that game, find out the final score, go to "that" site.

But we can be assured that there is hope for change. Jesus is here, ready, waiting, beckoning us with His mercy that is more powerful and more wonderful than any human-made device or service. Jesus has already solved the problem of our sinful behavior. Even if we slide right down that chute to sin again and again, He is there with His open arms of love, forgiveness, hope, and comfort. We're not doomed, we're not condemned to hell, we're not beyond help even when we can't keep ourselves from spiraling downward. We have hope because in His mercy, God sent Jesus to save us from sin and damnation—once and for all. God sent His Word, which is filled with the promise of forgiveness through Christ. And God sends people to help us along the way, guide us, keep us accountable, confront us when we need it, and love us in spite of ourselves. We have hope because we have God.

May this book offer you assurance of that when you need it most.

Hope

Dear Father in Heaven,

Yes, I'm calling You Father today. You have the strength, the wisdom, and the understanding I need as I struggle. I trust You as a good heavenly Father.

I know I am weak. I see that every day as I face temptation. I see my weakness in the track record I've established. But I have hope in You today.

Thank You, Father, for listening to me. Thank You for giving me the promise of the forgiveness of my sins—my many and dark sins. Thank You for letting me know that I'm not washed up. I'm not ruined. You still love me and You give me new life.

Please work in me so I will do what You want me to do. Please live in me so my actions will be pure and pleasing to You. Please fill me with Your Spirit so I can resist temptation and stop abusing technology. You're my Father in heaven. You know how to overcome this struggle. You know how to create a new heart in me. I have hope in You, God. Please help me, in Jesus' name.

Something to think about

Therefore, if anyone is in Christ, he is a new creation; the old has passed away; behold, the new has come.

2 Corinthians 5:17

I Confess

Dear God,

You've reminded me that You want me to come to You with my deepest struggles. You have a strong desire to carry my burdens. In fact, You already carried them to the cross on Jesus' shoulders. In my swirl of guilt and shame, it is so easy for me to forget that You are my Savior. You're even here to save me from my struggle with poor choices on the Internet.

There, I've said it. I've got a problem. I may not be able to be honest with anyone else right now, but I will be honest with You. I am abusing the Internet and accessing images, videos, and online chats that are not pleasing to You. That's an understatement. What I'm doing is ugly, crude, and demeaning. It's violent and wrong.

Telling You this doesn't make me feel any better, but I need to tell You. I need to be honest with You. I need to confess.

I'm not asking You to look the other way. I don't expect You to look upon me with any favor because I've been honest. I'm just asking for Your mercy. Please don't exclude me from Your promise of forgiveness. All I can hang on to is Your kindness, forgiveness, and grace. Please don't give me what I deserve. Instead, please help me out of this mess. Please forgive me, God. Please. And please free me from this prison. I know You can. Please, God, forgive me and help me.

Something to think about

If we claim to be without sin, we deceive ourselves and the truth is not in us. If we confess our sins, [God] is faithful and just and will forgive us our sins and purify us from all unrighteousness.

1 John 1:8–9 (NIV)

ONE DAY AT A TIME

Dear God,

It has become very clear to me that I must live from moment to moment, one day at a time, in Your strength and care. If I try to look too far ahead, I get overwhelmed. If I worry about what will happen later today or tomorrow, I lose track of Your grace, help, and direction for this moment.

I remember praying, "Give us this day our daily bread," in the Lord's Prayer. I think I have a deeper understanding of that phrase these days. My job is not to worry about the future. My calling is to trust You daily with my life because You are the trustworthy provider of all I need. I need to stop trying to be God and, instead, I need to rely completely on You.

This is not easy. But I'm being fed by Your Word. I never realized how helpful the Bible is. The strength and help it brings is beyond what I could have predicted. Thank You for sustaining me with Your life-giving truth.

I'll keep going one day at a time, depending

on You, celebrating Your forgiveness, love, and grace in my life. I will keep talking to You in prayer and listening for You in Your Word.

I'll never be perfect on this side of heaven. But with You each day, I am forgiven.

Something to think about

The steadfast love of the LORD never ceases; His mercies never come to an end; they are new every morning; great is Your faithfulness.

Lamentations 3:22–23

Fallen . . . Again

Dear God,

I'm ashamed to say it. I don't even feel worthy enough to speak with You right now. I've failed. I've fallen again.

Everything seemed to be going better. I felt strong. I felt free. I didn't even *want* to do what I did. But I was alone. I felt the strong desire. I just wanted to take a quick look, an innocent glance. An hour later I was in too deep. I feel like I'm back at square one. Why do You even bother to listen to me? I can barely last for twenty-four hours.

It is so easy for me to drift far from You, God. I know I can't be perfect, but why can't I do better? Why do I continue to disappoint You, myself, and the people around me? Why would You even want to stick with a loser like me?

Are You tired of me, God? I'm tired of myself. Can You love me more than I can love myself? I would answer that question with a no, but for some reason You answer that question with a yes. I am the prodigal son who has run off to a faraway place, living my life in sin. But You are the compassionate father, running to greet me, welcoming me back home. How I need Your open arms now, God. I don't deserve to be called Your slave, but You call me a son.

I've failed, but I am glad You are who You are.

Something to think about

"But while [the son] was still a long way off, his father saw him and was filled with compassion for him; he ran to his son, threw his arms around him and kissed him. The son said to him, 'Father, I have sinned against heaven and against you. I am no longer worthy to be called your son.' But the father said to his servants, 'Quick! Bring the best robe and put it on him. Put a ring on his finger and sandals on his feet. Bring the fattened calf and kill it. Let's have a feast and celebrate. For this son of mine was dead and is alive again; he was lost and is found.'"

Luke 15:20–24 (NIV)

Tired of the Burden

Dear God,

I'm tired. I'm tired of trying to resist the temptation. I'm tired of keeping secrets. I'm tired of living in the shadows. I'm tired of putting on a happy, normal face while I know that behind the scenes I'm living out lustful fantasies.

But I crave the feeling, the rush, the climax. And then I hate myself. Then I'm ashamed.

God, I can't continue to tolerate the roller-coaster ride. My mind feels like it's captured by either my next plan to find images that excite me or my strategy to hide what I've done. Clear my history online, check my download file, try to find alternate ways to access what I want to find. This is an exhausting way to live. I don't know if I can carry this burden anymore.

How can I stop the desire, the habit, the need? Sometimes I feel like I've gained control. But then I crash again. I've tried to stop. There are some moments when I think I've beat it. For a while I feel like I'm free. But a late night alone, feeling tired and neglected, needing to unwind and experience some pleasure in an otherwise 24-7 life in demand, and I fall. Again.

I don't even know if I deserve to ask for help, God. I've failed. I've failed You. I've failed my loved ones. The frightening thing about this is that I know I will fail again.

I'm tired, God. Will you help me?

Something to think about

[Jesus said,] "Come to Me, all who labor and are heavy laden, and I will give you rest. Take My yoke upon you, and learn from Me, for I am gentle and lowly in heart, and you will find rest for your souls. For My yoke is easy, and My burden is light."

Matthew 11:28–30

Guilty

Dear God,

You are faithful when I am faithless. You think of me even when I forget about You. You are with me always.

I'm thankful for who You are, but I also feel very guilty. If You're with me always, then You see what I do. You watch what I watch. You witness my lust, my weakness, and my uncleanness. You know I am a sinner.

Not everyone knows, but I still feel guilty. I feel like a hypocrite at home. I am a dishonest person at church. I try to forget my actions when I'm with other people. I've become good at hiding my sin and pretending that everything is just fine, but it makes me miserable. It's not easy to walk around every day consumed by guilt and shame.

But today I read something that rocked my world. I read that Your forgiveness even removes guilt. That's what I need. I need complete forgiveness. I need a new beginning with the burden of guilt lifted from me. I can't make that happen, God, but I know You can. Jesus carried my guilt along with my sin. Please carry it away from me today.

Something to think about

Then I acknowledged my sin to You and did not cover up my iniquity. I said, "I will confess my transgressions to the LORD." And You forgave the guilt of my sin.

Psalm 32:5 (NIV)

I'm Embarrassed

Dear Savior,

You are the one who rescues me. On the tossing ocean of my life, You're the one who brings me to safety. You're the one who calms the storm.

But this struggle makes me feel so embarrassed. I confided in a friend today. I know he won't tell anyone else. He even confessed to his own struggles with the Internet. I was relieved to share my pain with someone I trust. It was good to bring this challenge out of the darkness and into the light. But now someone knows the truth: I don't have my life all together. I'm not the person everyone thinks I am. It's somewhat humiliating.

Thank You for leading me to this step of sharing. Thank You for a friend who cares and understands. He's going to check in with me, and I'll check in with him. We'll keep each other accountable. This will help me. It's an answer to prayer.

Please help me with my embarrassment. This is a humbling journey. I thought I was so strong. Even when I was living in denial, I could pretend I was strong. But now I've admitted my weakness to someone. You promise that You will lift up the humble. Please keep lifting me up. I am humbled. Please keep giving me Your strength.

Something to think about

Humble yourselves before the Lord, and He will lift you up.

James 4:10 (NIV)

Powerless

Almighty God,

This journey is teaching me how weak I am. I should have realized it long ago. I remember singing when I was a little kid:

> **Jesus loves me, this I know,**
> **For the Bible tells me so;**
> **Little ones to Him belong;**
> **They are weak, but He is**
> **strong.**

I realize my weakness more and more every day. I see with greater clarity how strong You are. I know You have power over my struggle. Your love is stronger than my lust. I need Your strength as I crumble so easily in powerlessness.

Seeing one provocative billboard while I am driving can make me think how I might be able to get to a computer so I can view more images that please me. That is how weak I am.

One glance at a magazine cover with a scantily dressed woman and the headline, "Ten Sex Secrets" sends me into scheming my next secret Internet rendezvous. That is how weak I am.

So God, please live up to Your name. Please be my strength. Please be almighty over my sin. You are my strength and my salvation. That's what the Bible says. Be the strength I need so desperately. I am weak, but You are strong. That is my hope and encouragement today.

Something to think about

The LORD is my strength and my shield; in Him my heart trusts, and I am helped; my heart exults, and with my song I give thanks to Him.

Psalm 28:7

Is Progress Possible?

Dear Good Shepherd,

I'm calling You this because I heard this Bible verse the other day:

> **[Jesus said,] "The thief comes only to steal and kill and destroy; I have come that they may have life, and have it to the full. I am the good shepherd. The good shepherd lays down his life for the sheep."**
>
> John 10:10–11 (NIV)

The verse made me realize that it is possible to experience progress in my struggle. It is possible for me to do better, to live life more fully. It is possible to be brought away from the forces that steal, kill, and destroy my soul, into safe and nourishing pastures with You.

It is possible because You are the Shepherd who leads me and cares for me. You bring me from one place to another. You take me out of dangerous places and bring me to safe havens.

That is what I need from You, Jesus. I need You to carry me on Your shoulders back to the place that is best for me. I need You to bring me to a healthy place. I need You to make me whole again. I need You to be my Good Shepherd.

Someone told me that in Baptism we're buried with You into death, so that just as You were raised from the dead, we may also live a new life. Well, I've been baptized. Dear Jesus, Good Shepherd, bring me into the green pasture of living a new life.

Something to think about

The Lord is my shepherd; I shall not want. He makes me lie down in green pastures. He leads me beside still waters. He restores my soul. He leads me in paths of righteousness for His name's sake.

Psalm 23:1–3

My Relationships

Dear God,

I need help with my relationships. Getting wrapped up in a virtual world of lust and corruption has made me numb and passionless. My attention gets clouded. My feelings of sincere love and my ability to connect with people close to me have become strained and stilted. I feel like I've lost the real me.

You created me, God. You created love—real love. Please fill my heart with Your authentic love so I can invest in the people You have placed in my life. I want to be fully present. I want to be a good listener. I want to show healthy and genuine affection. But I can't do it when I'm empty. Please fill me with Your love so I can show it to the precious people around me.

I thank You for opening my eyes and heart to the reality of being Your new creation. I thank You for giving me a new chance every day. I thank You for Your forgiveness and for

Your love for me. I thank You that Jesus' death and resurrection open the door for my own new life.

Now I need You to fill me up with that newness. I can't be a faithful and compassionate person to others without Your faithfulness and compassion to me. Renew my heart, dear God. In doing so, please renew my relationships.

Something to think about

Create in me a clean heart, O God, and renew a right spirit within me. Cast me not away from Your presence, and take not Your Holy Spirit from me. Restore to me the joy of Your salvation, and uphold me with a willing spirit.

Psalm 51:10–12

Betrayal

Dear God,

I told my wife about my problem and asked her to come to a counselor with me.

My wife was devastated. She felt totally betrayed and hurt. I begged for mercy and apologized profusely. She is seeking counsel about what to do.

I'm so sorry that I haven't been a good steward of my marriage. You blessed me with a wife and, instead of investing in her, I sought fantasies and temporary thrills. Please forgive me, God. Please move my wife's heart to begin forgiving me. I've hurt her deeply and violated her trust. I don't expect her to trust me right now, but please open her heart so she knows that I love her and want to do better. I'm sorry I've placed this burden on her. Please strengthen her and relieve her pain. I know it's my fault.

During this journey I have seen that You are a God of mercy and grace. You love me even though I don't deserve it. You give me a new day and a new chance instead of condemnation. Please bring Your light and life into the darkness of my betrayal. Please nourish and support my wife's heart and soul.

I depend on Your goodness and Your restoring work, gracious God.

Something to think about

But You, O Lord, are a God merciful and gracious, slow to anger and abounding in steadfast love and faithfulness.

Psalm 86:15

Accountability

Dear God,

I remember that You are called the Wonderful Counselor, the Mighty God, and Prince of Peace. Those Christmas verses mean a lot to me right now. I need a Wonderful Counselor. In fact, I'm seeing a counselor today—and my wife has agreed to come along.

Thank You for this ray of hope. Thank You for allowing Your mercy to flow through her in a small way. Help me to honor this gift and new chance.

Most of all, I ask that the counselor will be someone I will be honest with and open to. I need help. I cannot break my lustful habits on my own. At this point in my life, it seems like they are deeply programmed into me. My default is to seek relief and excitement on the Internet. I am drawn to it. But when I fulfill my desire, I am crushed again.

I trust that You have provided help for me, opened the door to healthy dialogue about my sin, and brought me this far on the journey. Please don't stop Your healing work now. Please complete the work You have started in me.

I am amazed that what I thought was an insurmountable hidden problem crippling my life has come to light as an issue You can handle well. My fears about total rejection and destruction have been shown to be false. Yes, I am humbled, but You are lifting me up. You are strengthening me. Keep me on the path of healing and wholeness. Be my Wonderful Counselor!

Something to think about

For to us a child is born, to us a son is given; and the government shall be upon His shoulder, and His name shall be called Wonderful Counselor, Mighty God, Everlasting Father, Prince of Peace.

Isaiah 9:6

The Fight

Dear God,

I'm not out of the woods yet. Oh, the feelings of temptation are so strong! I want to give in. I crave the feeling. I am torn. What I want to do, I can't do. What I don't want to do, I end up doing. Please help me and deliver me, dear God!

There is a battle inside of me. I realize that I'm not the one doing the fighting. This is a fight between good and evil. I understand that You are fighting for me. I'm asking You to fight hard and fight strong. I don't want to be taken captive by lust and unfaithfulness.

For the first time, I am beginning to understand that good and evil are not equal competitors. You are good, and You are stronger than evil. You have even conquered death. Jesus has won the victory, and He is the one fighting for me. This is amazing news. It's a relief as I face each moment of my own strong and misguided sexual desires. You are stronger than my sin, and You have chosen to contend for my life.

All I can do is to ask You to keep waging the battle, God. Transcend my feelings with Your faithfulness. Don't let me do what I want to do, what my flesh craves and even enjoys. Take hold of me so that my life becomes a reflection of who You are.

Something to think about

I have been crucified with Christ. It is no longer I who live, but Christ who lives in me. And the life I now live in the flesh I live by faith in the Son of God, who loved me and gave Himself for me.

Galatians 2:20

The Long Haul Struggle

Dear God,

This is going to be a long haul. I've realized that this struggle may never go away. This may be my "thorn in the flesh," my weak point, my vulnerability.

It's difficult to admit that I have a specific weakness in my life. I always thought I was a strong person. I imagined that I would get stronger and stronger as I grew older. Now I see the truth. I have a glaring weakness that will probably be a part of my life until the day I die. This is a hard truth.

But I thank You for showing me the hard truth. Being made aware of my personal weakness and vulnerability allows me to ask You for specific help. It also allows me to order my life in a way that creates strong boundaries against failure.

Thank You for practical tools like Internet filters and accountability software. Thank You for providing people who can direct me and support the change process. Thank You for options that prevent me from accessing inappropriate material on my phone. Thank You for new options that lead me to wholeness in my life.

I don't like that I have to live in this guarded way. I don't enjoy living in weakness and admitting that I have a problem. But You are giving me a new sense of freedom as I face the truth. Take me by the hand and lead me on this long journey, gracious Savior. Because of Your strength and love, I'm ready to endure.

Something to think about

Give thanks to the LORD, for He is good, for His steadfast love endures forever.

Psalm 136:1

Should I Give Up?

Dear God,

Life is not going well. I've hurt some people, and they're angry with me. I've disappointed people close to me, and our relationships are not the same right now. I seem to be getting a lot of condemnation. Am I going to hell because of my Internet abuse?

I feel like I've committed the unforgiveable sin. But then I remember what my counselor said, "While we were sinners, Christ died for us." My sin is not unforgiveable. My sin is what You sent Jesus to die for and forgive. You know how broken I am. I am truly sorry for what I've done. I am doing everything I can to change. But I need Your strength because I am too weak.

I'll be honest, God. There are times when I feel like I want to give up. There are times when it feels like it was easier to live in secret than it is to face the truth and try to live in purity. But I will trust You. Even when I feel like throwing in the towel, even when I feel like going back to my old ways, You are with me to strengthen me and assure me that living for You is worth it. Living in freedom is where You call me to be.

By Your grace, I'll keep going.

Something to think about

Let us not become weary in doing good, for at the proper time we will reap a harvest if we do not give up.

Galatians 6:9 (NIV)

I Live by Grace

Dear Savior,

You are amazing. You forgive and pardon me even though I don't deserve it. You suffered and died for me even though I am no hero. You rose from the dead to give me new life even though I live so eagerly in my old life.

Thank You for being so good and so kind, dear Jesus.

Today I realize how I live completely by Your grace. You love and cherish me. Me! I don't deserve this lavish love at all. During this struggle with my sinful behavior online, You have extended Your hand of help and restoration. I am awed by how much You care about me. Even when I fail and am faithless, You come through with faithfulness and the gift of a second chance.

Thank You for being so generous and patient, dear Jesus.

This struggle has caused me to realize that my whole life is a life filled with Your grace.

From my birth and Baptism to this very day, I live by Your grace.

Thank You for keeping me around, sustaining me with Your love, and being who You are, dear Jesus.

Something to think about

For by grace you have been saved through faith. And this is not your own doing; it is the gift of God, not a result of works, so that no one may boast.

Ephesians 2:8–9

I Want to Follow

Dear God,

I want to follow You, but it is very difficult. I want to be pure, but it's hard to imagine living without my online "fixes." Even if I succeed for a little while, how do I know I won't go back? Even though I show my loved ones I'm trustworthy, how do I know I won't disappoint them and violate their trust again?

I believe that the help You've been giving me and the pathway of purity You have me on are good and healthy directions to take. But sometimes I want to go my own way. I want to pull up a sensual Web site and feel those feelings again.

The battle is raging, and it is exhausting. I feel like the man in the Bible who said, "I believe; help my unbelief!"

So, that's my prayer to You today, God. Help my unbelief. Help me when I don't know how to be helped. Lead me when I feel like I want to stray. Be my strength for good when I am leaning toward crumbling in weakness and impurity.

You call me to follow You, dear Savior. Draw me to Yourself. I can only follow You if You take hold of me and lead me. And in being led by You, I know I will have life.

Something to think about

No one can come to Me unless the Father who sent Me draws him. And I will raise him up on the last day.

John 6:44

The Way

Dear God,

Your kindness has led me to repentance. I understand that now. You have shown me my sin. You have exposed my guilt. You have led my heart to sorrow instead of resistance. You have turned me back to You for forgiveness. You are changing my life.

Thank You for loving me enough to provide a way out of this sin. I haven't overcome my Internet abuse. I understand that this will be a long journey. But You have brought me to a new place. Thank You for putting up with me—more than that, for loving me. Thank You for caring so much about my life that You deal with me in a truthful and merciful way.

Thank You for people in my life who care about me and support me in my weakness. Thank You for a counselor who is helping me along the way. Thank You for everything You are doing to free me from the oppressive bondage of darkness, secrecy, and shame. You are good to me.

The way ahead looks long and difficult, but I know I do not travel alone. You are with me. Even more than Your comforting presence, I know that You are the Way, the Truth, and the Life. My journey ahead will never take You by surprise, and You will lead me to wholeness and restoration forever.

Please stay with me, dear God. Never let me go.

Something to think about

For I am sure that neither death nor life, nor angels nor rulers, nor things present nor things to come, nor powers, nor height nor depth, nor anything else in all creation, will be able to separate us from the love of God in Christ Jesus our Lord.

Romans 8:38–39

My Strength

Dear God,

I praise You for who You are and for all You have done. From being my Creator to being my Savior, You show how much You treasure me and care for me.

I am deeply grateful for Your faithfulness toward me even when I stray from You. I am also thankful that You don't reject me when I commit shameful and ugly sins. My lust does not repel you. Instead You draw close to me to restore and help me.

Thank You for the compassion shown me by people You have placed in my life. I have hurt some people very deeply. I know that it will take a long time to restore trust. But You have extended kindness through so many. My words cannot express my thankfulness to You for Your patient and long-suffering spirit in my life.

As I move forward, I do so upon the foundation of the forgiveness of my sins, the strength I receive from You alone, and the certain hope of Your presence and care. I do not depend on myself, but on You and on the people You have placed in my life who keep me accountable and who help me.

Please lead me never to take Your grace for granted. Continue to work Your new life in me through Your Word and Sacraments. O God, be my strength and staying power for each day ahead.

Something to think about

Let us draw near to God with a sincere heart and with the full assurance that faith brings, having our hearts sprinkled to cleanse us from a guilty conscience and having our bodies washed with pure water. Let us hold unswervingly to the hope we profess, for He who promised is faithful. And let us consider how we may spur one another on toward love and good deeds.

Hebrews 10:22–24 (NIV)

General Prayers

Lord's Prayer

Our Father, who art in heaven, hallowed be Thy name, Thy kingdom come, Thy will be done on earth as it is in heaven. Give us this day our daily bread; and forgive us our trespasses as we forgive those who trespass against us; and lead us not into temptation, but deliver us from evil. For Thine is the kingdom and the power and the glory forever and ever. Amen.

Morning Prayer

I thank You, my heavenly Father, through Jesus Christ, Your dear Son, that You have kept me this night from all harm and danger; and I pray that You would keep me this day also from sin and every evil, that all my doings and life may please You. For into Your hands I commend myself, my body and soul, and all things. Let Your holy angel be with me, that the evil foe may have no power over me. Amen. (Martin Luther)

Evening Prayer

I thank You, my heavenly Father, through Jesus Christ, Your dear Son, that You have graciously kept me this day; and I pray that You would forgive me all my sins where I have done wrong, and graciously keep me this night. For into Your hands I commend myself, my body and soul, and all things. Let Your holy angel be with me, that the evil foe may have no power over me. Amen. (Martin Luther)

For Aid against Temptation

O God, You justify the ungodly and desire not the death of the sinner. Graciously assist us by Your heavenly aid and evermore shield us with Your protection, that no temptation may separate us from Your love in Christ Jesus, our Lord. (*LSB*, p. 312)

In Times of Temptation

Almighty and everlasting God, through Your Son You have promised us forgiveness of sins and everlasting life. Govern our hearts by

Your Holy Spirit that in our daily need, and especially in all time of temptation, we may seek Your help and, by a true and lively faith in Your Word, obtain all that You have promised; through the same Jesus Christ, our Lord. (*LSB*, p. 312)

For Purity

Almighty God, unto whom all hearts are open, all desires known, and from whom no secrets are hidden, cleanse the thoughts of our hearts by the inspiration of Your Holy Spirit that we may perfectly love You and worthily magnify Your holy name; through Jesus Christ, our Lord. (*LSB*, p. 312)

Suggested Scripture Readings

For Your name's sake,
O Lord, pardon my guilt,
for it is great. . . .
Turn to me and be gracious to me,
for I am lonely and afflicted.
The troubles of my heart are enlarged;
bring me out of my distresses.
Consider my affliction and my trouble,
and forgive all my sins. . . .
Oh, guard my soul, and deliver me!
Let me not be put to shame,
for I take refuge in You.
May integrity and uprightness
preserve me, for I wait for You.

Psalm 25:11, 16–21

Do not forsake me, O Lord!
O my God, be not far from me!
Make haste to help me,
O Lord, my salvation!

Psalm 38:21–22

God shows His love for us in that while we were still sinners, Christ died for us.

Romans 5:8

There is therefore now no condemnation for those who are in Christ Jesus. For the law of the Spirit of life has set you free in Christ Jesus from the law of sin and death. For God has done what the law, weakened by the flesh, could not do.

Romans 8:1–3

If we confess our sins, He is faithful and just to forgive us our sins and to cleanse us from all unrighteousness.

1 John 1:9